Life In The House By The Creek

A Collections Of Poems

By Charlie N. Wilson

Dedication

I dedicate this book to my wife Michele whose encouragement is constant and her praise never ending. She makes loving her easy. I could not do what I do without her.

Charlie Wilson

Copyright © 2017 All rights reserved.
Published by Charlie N. Wilson in the United States
ISBN-13: 978-1544913421
ISBN-10: 1544913427

Life in The House By the Creek is printed as a First Edition and made possible by a one-time gift-in-kind offer from Wayne Drumheller, Editor and Founder, The Creative Short Book Writers' Project for book and cover design, layout and formatting, editing assistance.

Printing Platform CreateSpace.
Amazon.com worldwide distribution

Introduction

"The roots of my raising run deep I come back for the strength that I need
And hope comes no matter how far down I sink the roots of my raising run deep"

Lyrics by Tommy Collins from the song "The Roots Of My Raising" performed by Merle Haggard

This is a collection of poems about growing up number six of twelve children in a house by the creek in the nineteen fifties and sixties in the south. These poems are about the people, places and events that shaped not only my life but those of my eleven brothers and sisters. Our family was a close knit bunch of rowdy kids with loving parents who didn't always give us what we wanted but always made sure we got what we needed. The basics: full tummies, clean clothes, a warm dry place to sleep and oh yeah, a whupping when called for. A home full of love, not often spoken but always present. We were the lucky ones. Learning early what was right and what was wrong. Lessons that shaped and molded us to become whatever we chose to be. These poems are dedicated to them, my Mother and Daddy and my five sisters and six brothers.

I wouldn't have the dreams I do without them.

CONTENT

Photo 1955
First row L-R: Tony, Mother, Baby Vanessa, Dad, Scotty,
Stephen, Stephanie
Second row L-R: Mike, Gary, Linda, Charlie
Third row L-R: Brenda, Benny, Bobbie

A Modest Home

Sitting by the creek it was a modest home
plenty of room for two kids to roam.
Another year and there were three
It's getting crowded on Daddy's knee.

Time flies when you're having fun
Add three more - six now - we're done.
Not so fast came the voice from heaven
Take a deep breath there will soon be seven.

Summon Grandpa with his hammer and saw
Raise the roof add rooms for all.
Eight and nine came right on time
twins they were, made Mom's heart shine.

Ten then eleven is there no end?
The light in the tunnel is just round the bend.
Doc told Mom it was time to stop
an even dozen would round the lot.

Sitting by the creek was a
modest home
plenty of room for twelve
kids to roam.

April 2016

1

Round the House by the Creek

Round the house by the creek on the outskirts of
town
The air was cool, leaves covered the ground.
A special day was about to break,
number six was born now a family of eight.

Round the house by the creek the years added up
The family grew - six more was enough.
Round the house by the creek when the snow hit
the ground
The kids inside were all standing around.

Backs to the wood stove toasting their buns
Turn around now your butts are well done.
Patience is a virtue so I've been told
Waiting for the bathroom is getting kind of old.

In the kitchen the windows were covered with fog
From the steam off the biscuits ready for all.
Round the house by the creek all through those
years
We cried some tears and smiled ear to ear.

Battles were fought and loves were lost,
Hearts broken and mended we managed it all.
Round the house by the creek as the years passed
by
Each one took their turn at trying to fly.

The nest is now empty they've all flown away
To raise their own families the old fashioned way.

Round the house by the creek on the outskirts of town
You can feel your love ones walk over the ground.

The air is still but holds love none the less
To pass on to others as they build their nests.

December 2014

Down The Road

Down the road just out of town
next to the creek on a small piece of ground
was a learning place for twelve kids and a dog,
a snake or two and an occasional frog.

Growing up is a lot of fun when all you need is a
place to run.
Thru the woods and in the creek the games we
played were hard to beat.
Baseball in the summer, football in the fall, kick
the can we did it all.
Tobacco stick horses tied to a tree, a fort in the
woods where you wanted to be
when the BB gun aimed at your gut missed its
mark and hit your butt.

Bullfrog houses built in the sand on the banks of
the creek
where the fish hawks stand.
Rabbit tobacco in a corn cobb pipe
will make you sick if it ain't done right

A trip to the river took all day
but it wasn't the very best place to play.
Down the sawdust pile at the old saw mill
in the hood of a car, boy what a thrill.

A big Coke ®sign from the swimming pool road
makes a great sled in the deep winter snow.
Twelve kids and a dog played just out of town
next to the creek on a small piece of ground.

January 2014

The Big Tree

Down by the creek on a hot summer day
The ole big tree was the place we played.
Water ran about three feet deep
Horny head suckers nibbled our feet.

Momma's straight pins bent like a hook
With a little ball of bread that's all it took
To catch those suckers and a brim or two
Catch and release was the right thing to do.

Down by the creek on this hot summer day
The ole big tree has since gone away.
Though it lives on forever in our memories today
The ole big tree was the place we played.

March 2015

The Country Store

On top of the hill half mile from the creek,
was an old country store where the farmers would
meet.
They came every night round seven o'clock,
talked world affairs and this year's crops.

Merita ® bread sign on the squeaky screen door,
oil and sawdust on the pine board floor.
Gas pumps out front, kerosene too
filled Dad's old truck for a buck or two.

Coal in a sack by the front door
fed the little black stove in the middle of the floor.

Cane back chairs, ale crates on end,
formed a circle around that black bundle of tin.

Douglas Edwards gave the news of worldly affairs,
but those in the circle didn't much care.

Ole' Ike played golf was the news of the day,
must be nice to be living that way.

Thirty five cents was all the cash they had
but with a good wife and kids - life wasn't so bad.
Ice in the drink box, candy in the jars,
credit slips in the cash drawer your word took you
far.

The sound of a cat was always around
though the little fur ball could never be found.
Over here, no over there, didn't matter much
when all you had was the sound and a hunch.

The sawmill was buzzn' just down the road,
toten' slabs in the heat was more than a load.
Whistle blows - time to break
lunch in a bag on an old Pepsi® crate.

An ice cold drink was more than a treat
from the ole country store where the farmers
would meet.
Deposit on the drink bottles two cents at the time
don't sound like much but we didn't mind.

It was summer in the south half mile from the creek at the ole country store where the farmers would meet.
Time moves on, sixty years have passed
Half mile from the creek is now all grass.

January 2014

Mother

She was up every morning at the break of day
gave us biscuits and gravy we were on our way.
Her attention would turn to the chores of the day
washing and ironing, no time to play
Lunch for Dad was always at noon
stories at three would come on soon
Search for Tomorrow, The Edge of Night
her rest time over, school bus in sight.
Front door bangs open, books thrown on the couch
we head for the kitchen to wonder about
No need for snacks she would always say
spoil your supper now go out and play.
Dad gets home at half past five
she would be at the stove fixin' chicken to fry.
Peach cobbler in the oven made the house smell
sweet
Mashed potatoes and gravy were hard to beat
Supper was over the dishes all washed
she cleaned off the table to make us a spot
Homework to us seemed such a chore
but we didn't know she had already done more
Time for bed the sheets are all clean
now say your prayers and forgive those mean
She was up every morning at the break of day
gave us biscuits and gravy we were on our way.

January 2014

Fuzzy

He was a ball of fur, didn't weigh 3 pounds,
When Daddy brought him home from Henderson
town.
It was winter time the weather was cold
So he slept in a shoe box behind the wood stove.
So cute and cuddly, all warm and cozy.
What should we name him, what about Fuzzy?
Spring came soon, followed by summer.
Fuzzy grew bigger and the days got warmer.
"OK kids the time has come.
He's an outside dog needs to play in the sun."

He was never trained to do any tricks
He had no interest in fetching a stick.
Though never assigned, his job on the place
Was to make sure that we were all safe.
Cows and pigs, ducks and chickens,
All knew their place or they'd take a licking.

I was out in the yard when the dog catcher came
round
Said Fuzzy had no collar must go to the pound.
With a tear in my eye I sounded the alarm.
Momma's at the back door with a broom on her
arm.
I looked up at her she looked down at me
She put her hand on my head, pulled me close to
her knee.
"Don't fret now it'll be alright
Fuzzy will sleep on the front porch tonight."
She pointed that broom at the man in the truck
"The dog stays here so don't push your luck.
Awfully good of you to stop, but you can't stay.
Best you go now – so be on your way."
The message he got was loud and clear
As he backed out of the drive we all gave a cheer.
The days that followed turned into years.
Uncle Sam called for me and I left in tears.
The years away were not so bad
Until a letter from home made my heart sad.
That ball of fur we still love today
After 14 years had passed away.

February 2014

Barefoot

The first of May was the official day
Momma let us put our shoes away.
School will be out in less than a week
We'd roll up our britches and head for the creek.

The tender skin on the bottom of your toes
Feels funny at first but everyone knows
That it won't be long before you could run
Over a road of gravel and not feel a one.

The grass in the front yard is starting to grow
The clover's white blooms are beginning to show.
Filled with pollen just right for the taking
The honey bees gather for the honey they're
making.

A walk thru the clover is no fairy book tale
When you step on a bee, he stings, you yell.
Momma pulls out the stinger, rubs some liniment
on, the swelling is starting but soon will be gone.

"You'll be OK by the end of the day
Now be on your way, go on and play."
It's back to the creek and the chores at hand
Building toy boats and castles in sand.

You gotta have wood to build a good boat
So it's off to the scrap pile to get all you can tote.

Careful now those planks have nails
OOPS too late, you let out a yell.

You limp back to the house no running for sure
Where Momma is ready with her homemade cure.
A call to the doctor, not on your life
A piece of salt pork will make it alright.

She put it on the hole where the nail broke the skin.
Wrapped it tight with a rag, "Now go play again."
She kept a watchful eye to see progress was made.
If the pork did its job you would be OK.

In a day or two the soreness is gone
Now go play again, what else can go wrong.
Summer flies by, things change like the weather
By the end of the summer our feet were like leather.

All crusty and tan and hard as a rock
Now our shoes won't fit not even the socks.
Roll down your britches, say goodbye to the creek
School will be starting in less than a week.

Summer was fun we wished it could stay
And the first of May is so far away.

April 2015

Holy Ground

Riding down the two lane road
I can see the proud old home
Standing stately by the creek
Where as a child I roamed
Pulling in the drive way
I gaze across the creek
At the rocky hill where Daddy plowed
The food we had to eat
As the memories stir inside my head
I slowly look around
My soul is turning in my chest
This is truly holy ground
One by one the pictures flash
Before my teary eyes
Of a way of life we loved back then
But now has all but died
A summer Sunday afternoon with all the kids
around playing "*kick the can*" on truly holy ground
The sun sets low across the creek
The air is cooling down
Daddy cut a watermelon and passed it all around
One by one the pictures flash before my teary eyes
Of a way of life we loved back then
But now has all but died

March 2016

The inspiration for this story came from Merle Haggard's
"The Roots Of My Raising" Lyrics by Tommy Collins

Shucking Corn

Early September was a special time
Shucking corn was a favorite of mine.
Ole Bill hitched, to the field we would go
Didn't come back til we had a wagon load.
Kin folk gathered from all around
To shuck all the corn piled high on the ground.
The grown-ups would sit in a circle around
That mountain of corn piled high on the ground.
A long table was made with boards from the barn
Covered with cloth, time to sound the alarm.
Slow down now - don't be too quick
All the foods not out yet and put down that stick.
Kids running around, dog chasing the cat
Good friends and kin folk what's better than that?

April 2014

Mr. Ben

Early each morning as the sun came up
he would drive down the hill in his pickup truck.
Two toots on the horn and we all knew
it was time to get up and shake off the dew.

I looked out the window as he drove up the road
to the store on the hill where the farmers would go.
A lean sorta fella, soft spoken and kind
Mr. Ben was his name, that's all we knew at the
time.

Things started to stir in the house by the creek
Mom in the kitchen fixin' something to eat.
Biscuits in the oven soon ready to eat
country ham frying, boy what a treat.

Scrambled eggs and gravy would round out the
meal some of Grand Paw's molasses would seal
the deal.
Sister Bobbie was dressing for work downtown
while the rest of us were just stumbling around.
Some cold water on your face would shock you
awake most of the time that's all it would take.

After breakfast was done we were ready to go
"Hurry up kids, get on with the show."
Mr. Ben would come back and with any luck
we'd all be ready to jump in his truck.

The ride to the barn was a rocks throw away
A short one for sure to start a long hard day.
With mule hitched to sled we'd head to the field
to pull all the tobacco the poor ground could yield.

First sled full, its back to the barn
black snake in the path won't do any harm.
But the mule gets spooked and starts to run
sled turns over - that load is done.

Sister Brenda at the table tying tobacco on sticks,
to pick up her speed she tries a few tricks.
Works well for a while that's all it would take
for lunch time is soon, we all need a break.

And so it goes for the rest of the day
long into the evening we all had to stay.
Tobacco all tied and hung in the barn
a hard day of work never did any harm.

Mr. Ben would come back and with any luck
we'd all show up and jump in his truck.
The ride to the house was a rocks throw away
a short one for sure to end a long day.

January 2014

Making Molasses

What we called the old cane mill
Sat just above the creek on the side of a hill.
The big red tractor with a belt a mile long
Turned the huge wheel, now what could go wrong.

Turns out a plenty if she ain't lined up right
The belt would fly off, boy what a site.
Two giant rollers, one on top of the other
Pressed the juice from the cane, was the color of
butter.

A pan at the bottom caught the juice from above
Flowed down in a trough, and filled the cook tub.
Start the fire and bring it up to the boil
Keep stirring and skimming don't let it spoil.

The fire is popping there's plenty of steam
As it starts to cook the color is green.
Hour by hour we continue the chore
I'm just a kid and my back's getting sore.

The fire is pulled when the color turns black
Let it cool down slow, keep stirring don't slack.
When it finally cools down it's the end of the day
Bring up the jars let's put it away.

The tub is empty but before we start moppin'
Bring on the biscuits - the fun part was soppin'.

April 2014

Smoking at the Big Tree

From the back kitchen door Mom could see up the
creek to the big oak tree where often we'd meet.
One summer afternoon bout half past three
four siblings were bunched at the base of that tree.

The tree was huge, grew out over the water
made a diving platform when the days got hotter.
Dad kept his smokes on top of the hutch
taking two packs didn't take much.

That's where we gathered with cigarettes in hand
to puff our brains out, throw the butts in the sand.

From the kitchen back door Mom could see up the
creek to the big oak tree where we decided to
meet.

The smoke was a risin' from the base of the tree
They were all smokin', the exception was me.
We ranged in ages from five to ten
seems such a young age to be dabbling in sin.
Just so happens it was about time
for Dad to get home, he was right on time.
"The creek's on fire" was the cry from the door
when Dad came in sight we were smokin' no more.

Back to the house we were marched in a line
To pick our own switches, twas a matter of time.
Judgment day had arrived and punishment was
certain when all's said and done our butts would be
hurtin'.

As he came down the line with a grin on his face
I thought to myself this might be the place
to step out of line and plead my case.
It's a long shot - maybe, but I uttered these words

"Don't whip ME Daddy - I'm just a baby."

January 2014

Shelling Beans

After supper when the sun went down
We'd gather up baskets and all circle around.
Down by the creek where the air was cool
The task at hand required no tools.

Round in a circle we'd all take a spot
Bushels of beans in the center, sure looks like a lot.
Everybody get some put'em in your lap
Break off the ends and give them a snap.

Piece of cake nothing to this
Next bushel up was a whole new twist.
Butterbeans. Now that was a chore
Had to break 'em open made your fingers sore.

The night air filled with the smell of smoke
Burning burlap rags kept "skeeters" away- no joke.
Down by the creek where the air was cool
The task just finished required no tools.

May 2016

The Little White Church

At the top of the hill across from the store
sat the little white church, but so much more.
When Sunday morning came around
the sound of the bell could be heard clear to town.

Things were buzzin' in the house by the creek
Mom had us all washed and ready to eat.
Little short pants all cleaned and pressed
Buster Brown® shoes had to look their best.

Go the back way stay off the main road
Cut thru the yards where the footpath goes.
Johnny's house then on past Lynn's
Benny Ray's is round the next bend.

When you got to Aunt Carrie's you knew you were
done.
Now it's time to have some fun.
The rooms in the back were all kinda small
Felt boards and posters covered the walls.

Little tables and chairs sitting around
Drawers on the front where the crayons were
found.
Mrs. Bland was our teacher we loved her back then
She cuddled us all like an old mother hen.

There foundations were laid for the times that
would follow without her kind words our lives
would be hollow.
Looking back now I seem to recall
That Christmas time was the best of all.

Christmas Eve would always start
with the Christmas play, I forgot my part.
Front teeth are gone you're trying to speak
Whole body shaking clear down to your feet.

The sweat starts to collect on both your hands
When you glance to the left and see Mrs. Bland.
Your life just got better that instant in time,
the words came together and started to rhyme.

The worst part is over you conquered defeat
best parts ahead when they give you your treat.
A brown paper bag filled to the top
with apples and oranges, candy hard as a rock.

Bananas and raisins, tangerines too
All kinds of nuts just waiting for you.
Put your name on your bag so there won't be a
fuss, when we all get back home there's too many
of us.

Time for bed Santa's coming soon
He'll find his way by the light of the moon.
Over the top of the hill across from the store
Past the little white church and so much more.

January 2014

Momma's Daddy

Momma's Daddy as I recall

Was a big strapping man over 6 feet tall.

Work in the sun had weathered his brow

His hands big as baskets from holding the plow.

His long sleeve shirt buttoned clear to his neck

He would sit on a bucket and watch his chickens peck.

Work came easy for him and Ole Bill

The one eyed draft horse that turned the cane mill.

It was late in the evening that summer day

Ole Bill was pulling a big wagon of hay.

The drive lines were slack Ole Bill couldn't know

The wheel of the wagon hit the road ditch below.

"Git up " he shouted, Ole Bill strained the lines.

The wagon was stuck but in a short time,

The pitch fork was jabbed in Ole Bill's behind.

That bit of encouragement was all it took

Ole Bill jerked that wagon about ten foot.

A big strapping man over six feet tall

Quoted the Bible when sober for one and for all.

His kids called him Papa, he had a stern hand

Fair to say Momma's Daddy was a complex man.

February 2017

Dixon's Swimming Pool

When the sun hit the windows on the house by the creek
In less than two seconds we were on our feet.
Put on some shorts and maybe a shirt
Run down the stairs, stumped my toe- that hurt.

"Slow down kids you got all day
Wait till the water warms, then you can play."
Grab a biscuit and out the door we would run
To the top of the hill for a day full of fun.

Swim At Your Own Risk read the sign over the
gate
That didn't mean much we were only eight.
Aunt Annie was there opening up the drink stand
We'd all pitch in and give her a hand.

Ice down the drink box, put the nabs in the jars
Set up the checker board, find the Rook® cards.
Rake the sand by the pool, straighten up the chairs
Clean out the bath houses -they need the fresh air.

Chores are all finished a job well done
The water is warm now let's have some fun.
Snake in the gully was the game we played
Stayed under the water most of the day.

Lips are blue, skin is all wrinkled
Time to get out I need to tinkle.
Sun fades in the west behind the oak trees
Air cooling down I feel a shake in my knees.
Wrap a towel all around to capture some heat
Head to the drink stand to get something to eat.
Aunt Annie is busy closing up shop
But gives us some nabs and a soda pop.

The feeling is starting to come back in my feet
Time to go home to the house by the creek.

March 2013

Sweet Taste Of Summer

It was a sunny day in late July
when a Crimson Sweet caught my eye.
She was lying in a field
off the swimming pool road
I knew Mr. Pink wouldn't have to know.
Severs Creek flowed just below
to its cool clean water we had to go.

I picked her up to the creek we went
where I laid her down she was heaven sent.
She was my first to be taken that way
that sweet taste of summer is with me today.

I have tasted a lot since that day in July
but none better I cannot lie
BEST WATERMELON
I EVER HAD.

December 2013

Sounds Of A Summer Night

On a summer night in the house by the creek
All the windows were open to let out the heat.
The curtains would flutter as the breeze passed
thru, bringing sounds of the night plus a bug or
two.

A cricket would chirp, a bull frog croak,
Fuzzy would bark at the cars on the road.
But the sound I remember coming down from the
hill was the clanging of horseshoes steel against
steel.

If you lay real quiet you could pick out the words
Of the songs on the juke box loud enough to be
heard.
The good times were rolling at the top of the hill
The pavilion was rocking, many found their thrill.

From all around the young folks would gather
To dance to the music, sit around and chatter.
The Wurlitzer® Jukebox on the center right wall
Had a hundred tunes and we knew them all.

"Sixty Minute Man", *"Annie Had A Baby"*
and *"One Mint Julep"* were some of the favorites.
The lights in the trees lit the ground below
Around the steel stakes so the guys could throw.
For hours on end they would pitch on the hill

The clanging of horseshoes, steel against steel.

Aunt Annie in her drink stand served up the
snacks.
She had Pepsi® and Coke® and Cracker Jacks®.
Her checker board was always set up
To take on all comers – who would step up?

If you did be assured it wouldn't be long
Before you were done – time to move on.
Night turns to day and a new set of rules.
"Swim At Your Own Risk" at Dixon's Swimming
Pool.

March 2014

Let's you and me

Hitch the wagon boys we're going to town.
Gettin' over in the evening so don't fool around.
I've never been down this road before.
Who lives here? Who's that at the door?

What day is this, is it July?
Tomorrow's Thanksgiving, don't you smell those
pies?
What's your name, do I know you?
Was plowing yesterday the horse lost a shoe.

It's OK Dad I'm one of your boys.
Let's you and me go make some noise.
We'll call the cows, just bang on this bucket.
Feed them some corn no need to shuck it.

The garden looks good, tomatoes are ripe,
Squash full of blooms, ain't that a sight.
Got a new calf, she was born last night,
She's there in the barn all curled up tight.

Let's you and me go take a peek,
Careful where you step now, look down at your
feet.
Another day passes they add up to years
Eight I recall and a billion tears.

We watched him go down that mindless road
Often wondering- just what does he know.
In the end it really didn't matter
He knew where he was - though we felt sadder.

Let's you and me go down that road
Be a little more mindful of what we don't know.

March 2014

Grandpa's Girls

From her booster seat in Grandpa's "hick-up" truck
She had a bird's eye view of the chickens and
ducks.
Juicy Juice® and Cheerios®,
little pig tails with little pink bows.

Tiny cowgirl boots and a short denim skirt
a small teddy bear on the front of her shirt.
Dressed for the farm away we would go
Ride around easy, ride around slow
Today's only here for an hour or so.

"Millie goats" I recall she would say,
We're running around ready to play.
A miniature horse named "Lilo" stood by
with her baby that measured only 12 inches high.

Climb on the tractor mash the pedal and go
Ride around easy, ride around slow,
Today's only here for an hour or so.

School bell rings it's off to class
College years ending, sure was a blast.

Ride around easy, ride around slow
Today's only here for an hour or so.

The music is playing as we walk down the aisle
Her white gown flowing, draws nothing but
smiles.

Ride around easy, ride around slow
Today's only here for an hour or so.

From her booster seat in Great Grandpa's old truck,
she has a bird's eye view of the chickens and
ducks.

Ride around easy, ride around slow
Today's only here for an hour or so.

January 2013

Cheerleaders

It's Friday night the lights are bright
Stadium full student body on the right.
In a few more minutes its kick off time
Cheerleaders lining up on the fifty yard line.
Saddle oxfords with white bobbi socks,
skirts to the ankles don't show a lot.
About the game they don't know much
Who has the ball, what down and such.
Matters not to those on the squad
just be cute when given the nod.
The game has started wonder if they know
who has the ball, which way to go.
Things go well its field goal time
The cheer goes out they're all in a line.
"Block that kick" was the battle cry
Coach stops the play why doesn't he try.
He jumps the bench to confront the girls
the hair on his head is starting to curl.
"What the hell is the matter with ya'll
don't you know we have the damn ball"
To be a cheerleader you need not be a scholar
All one needs are the pipes to holler.

January 2014

*This is a true story told to me by my wife Michele. Just so
happens she was a cheerleader on that high school squad
in 1960.*

Highway To Heaven

On this highway to Heaven
We pass thru a lot
Of beauty and ugliness
Like it or not.

Designed by your hand
To test us each day
And more often than not
We can't find our way.

Yet still we move on
Uphill and down
To reach that rest stop
Too soon will be found.

The bumps in the road
Tear at our souls,
Heartache and sadness
Add to the load.

On this highway to heaven
We pass thru a lot
It's simply called life
Like it or not.

December 2016

It's 3am

It's 3am and I'm wide awake
the reason could be I went to bed at eight.
This schedule I'm on is taking its toll
The reason could be I'm just getting old.

After dinner each night I usually retire
to the TV room and the big leather chair.
I settle in who could ask for more
in less than ten minutes I'm starting to snore.

My partner for life comes into the room
she stands by the chair, is that a broom?
Oh no she wouldn't that broom's made for
sweeping
Even in my sleep I know what she's thinking.

I gently stir to give her a clue
so she'll know it ain't right what she's fixin' to do.
"Are you awake" she says with a poke?
"Just resting my eyes", now that was a joke.

I can see on her face that she has her doubts
So I pull off my blankie and try to get out.
Appears my legs didn't get the memo
next thing I know the floor's hitting my elbow.

She reaches down to help me get up
Over 200 pounds is a little too much.
Her balance is lost, she's out of control

I brace for the worst, the crash takes its toll.

Its 3am and I'm wide awake
The reason could be my whole body aches.

January 2014

My Wife

A special lady there is no doubt
I often wonder how I did without
such a caring person who can't be still
who talks too much and moves at will.

A thing of beauty in constant motion
and her butt still looks small beside the ocean.
I blessed the day that we were wed
my beer drinking buddies said I 'd lost my head.

No matter though it just felt right
after fifty years I saw the light.
The times in life when things don't work
she's right there to take on the hurt.

A better person there's none around
A partner for life I finally found.
A special lady there is no doubt
and one I'd rather not live without.

January 2014

Slept in the Yard

I woke up this morning with the sun in my eyes.
head hurt so bad I thought I would die.
I don't remember leaving that bar
shut the front door - I slept in the yard.

My eye site is fuzzy all I can see
Is three inches of grass looking back at me.
My mouth is so dry I want a drink
The hose is right here who needs a sink.

Hold on a minute what's that I hear
Shut the front door there's an ant in my ear.
This water I feel is sure out of place
Oh now I see the dog's licking my face.

On my knees I'm starting to focus
My pickup appears to be in motion.
Settle down just get a grip-my suitcase is here
Am I taking a trip?

Say it ain't true ya'll I can't go far
My clothes are scattered all over the yard.
I still don't remember leaving that bar
shut the front door - I slept in the yard.

January 2014

My Heart Hurts Today

My heart hurts today
a young family's mother was taken away.

Why them Lord what did they do
to receive what appears to be punishment from
You.

Young lives forever today will change
as they struggle with life - some cursing Your
name.

Those of us who are older in years
know the pain will pass as we fight back the tears.

Comfort them Lord do what You can
to heal their hearts so they again take Your hand.

Life ain't fair for sure that's true
So we hold on tight depending on You.

My heart hurts today for the young family
whose Mother was taken away.

February 2017

Turning Out The Lights

One by one Gods turning out the lights
The sound of that old juke box no longer fills the
nights.
A row of fools sat on those stools till dark turned
into light.
One by one Gods turning out the lights.

We rode'm hard in those smoke filled bars beneath
the neon lights, when all the while the ones at
home just longed to be held tight.

We had a time back in our prime some fifty years
ago the Hag wrote songs of the common man that
rocked us to our toes.

The answers to life's questions were seldom ever
found a familiar phrase cut thru that haze - bar
keep bring us one more round.
Just one more beer mixed with tears and we'll
leave it all behind.
The chairs are stacked, the party's over, we're all
but out of time.

A final glance, just one last chance to hold a
memory tight.
To feel the warmth from years ago - before God
turns out the lights.

December 2014

The Train Ride Home

I was sitting in the station waiting for my train
When an old worn out gentleman called out to me
- my name.

A stranger on that platform I never before knew
Wore a dirty coat, a frayed hat and holes in both
his shoes.

The way he looked it's safe to say - I'd wager you
a bet
He had ridden hard beneath the stars and always
laid up wet.

Uninvited he brushed the bench to make himself a
seat.
My eyes and nose conveyed to me his home was
on the street.

He settled in the best he could to share a line of
talk
"Been on the street for 60 years my legs don't like
to walk."

"I'm headed home one last time to visit the one I
love.
Gonna' place a rose on that marble stone with her
name beneath a dove."

His hand touched mine as he spoke those lines, his
eyes were filled with tears.
Off in the distance a whistle blows the train will
soon be here.

A sudden chill came over me, I felt it in my bones
60 years had come and gone since Dad left Mom
alone.

The train pulls in, I'm on my feet, not feeling quite
the same
From over my shoulder an old worn out gentleman
Calls out to me - my name.

January 2015

*The stories and poems that follow were
submitted by some of my sisters and brothers.
Since they played such a large part in my life in
the **House By The Creek** I thought it only
fitting that they also share their memories.*

The Island

In 1940 *The Island* was to the right and rear of our house by the creek. At that time *The Island* was a big hog lot and my older brother Benny and I would often peer over the fence and watch the hogs eat.

Over the next ten years Daddy gradually changed *The Island* into a place where family and friends would gather to celebrate birthdays or just have school friends over for a cookout. Daddy built a bridge across the creek, ran electric lights and constructed a brick grill, in those days called a "Dutch oven". Relatives, neighbors and friends would gather for fish fries and fun. As a teenager I would have hotdog parties for my school friends and Daddy would blink the lights at 9pm sharp to signal the party was over.

In 1955 Momma made a picture of me on *The Island* with siblings Stephanie, Stevie, Tony and baby Vanessa. That was my last year at home as I was getting married and moving out.

In the early sixties Daddy decided to fill in one side of the creek to make *The Island* part of the backyard. He would follow the state highway crews to get the dirt they pulled from the ditches. In those days the road by the house was dirt and gravel.

With the right side of the creek filled in the new backyard was now a hundred feet wider. My Daddy had vision, determination, patience and fortitude, traits he would pass on to his twelve children, well some of them.

Momma and I made raised planter beds and filled them with flowers and planted azaleas around some of the trees. The view from the kitchen windows looked like a picture from *Home and Garden* magazine.

Now almost 80 years later Momma and Daddy's great grandchildren play in the yard that was once a hog lot and later ***The Island***.

Bobbie Wilson Miles

Bobbie was the oldest daughter and we were told she was Daddy's favorite. Now that's the truth- according to Bobbie.

Our Personal Playground

Growing up in a house with a creek running by

Was an education for us that money couldn't buy.

We never knew just where the creek started,

But when it got to us, it so gently parted.

 Then there were two creeks in which we could play,

That's where we spent many fun hours each day.

We played in those creeks in our little bare feet,

What was normal for us- for our playmates a treat.

There were flowers and ferns and moss on the shore,

And beneath our wet feet there were rocks by the score.

And under those rocks we found life did exist.

There were crawfish and lizards, we could not resist.

Tadpoles and frog eggs were my favorite finds.

My Mason® jar full, better leave some behind.

I'd take them to school for my classmates to see.

They were all jealous and wanted to come home with me.

As the two creeks joined up at the opposite end

It created an island for family and friends.

Daddy had built our own little park.

With benches between trees, attached to the bark.

He made a "Dutch Oven," as his stone grill was called.

With hotdogs and burgers he fed one and all.

We had parties and cookouts on that island of ours,

Under blossoming Dogwoods like a canopy of flowers.

And when the days turned cool with the autumn breeze

I would work a full day raking up all the leaves.

But those piles were not burned - oh no indeed.

They became the walls of the rooms for my own house to be.

Just looking around, nature made much available

Wild flowers in jars on my Pepsi® crate table.

I worked so hard fixing everything just so,

Until Mama would call -- then it was time to go.

I loved my little houses I built on that land,

But the one I loved most, Daddy made with his hands.

Linda *"Gracie"* Wilson Gwaltney

Linda was a year older than me, married an Elon Graduate from Smithfield, Va., moved with him back to Va. and has two children who are now older than she was when she left home and are both Elon Graduates.

I can't remember why we called her "Gracie".

Memories

The fish intended never came
But it kept him at it just the same.
He'd stroll the pier from morn 'til night
Talking to any and all in sight.

Sometimes Mama was by his side
Until one day she cast and the whole rig said
goodbye.
I guess that ended her sport for the day
But surely gave Daddy plenty to say.

They'd always return to the scene in the fall
Until in their seventies poor health made it's call.
But oh what memories they had to share
Of fishing and camping, that now seem so rare.

So keep this old hook as another embrace
Of PawPaw and Granny….another time another
place.

Brenda Wilson Moser

*This poem written by sister Brenda was framed with a large
fish hook and given to her son and his family as **another
embrace of PAWPAW and Granny.***

*"One day I stopped by the house by the creek for no particular reason. As usual the door wasn't locked and I went inside. No one was home. Mom and Dad had gone on a trip to the beach, I think. I can't remember for sure. The house was empty and unusually quiet so I sat down and was letting my mind wonder about nothing in particular. As I thought about all the things that this house had been a part of, these words came to mind as if **the house was talking** to me. I found some paper and a pencil and wrote this poem/song in about thirty minutes. When I got home that evening I made some minor changes and **Wood and Stone** is the result of that experience.*

I'm sure that house still has some stories to tell."

Mike Wilson

Wood & Stone

Here I am alone again

They have gone away once more.

How I miss those little feet

Walking upon my wooden floors.

He worked the fields from early dawn

With no complaint of pain he spoke.

She cooked their meals and nursed the young

Just to make this house a home.

Without their presence here within

I am only wood and stone.

And that old tree that shades my face

Of secrets that it's limbs must hold.

Of the good and bad times they both shared

As together they're growing old.

But now his walk is bent and feeble

And her hair is turning gray.

He sits and wonders what will be

When heaven has called them both away.

I wish somehow there was a way

That I could let them know.

Without their presence here within

 I am only wood and stone.

My seasoned timbers bear the weight

They passed the test all through the years.

The emptiness of my lonely walls

Adds to the silence of my tears.

I wish somehow there was a way

That I could let them know.

Without their presence here within

 I am only wood and stone.

Mike Wilson

*This poem was rewritten by Mike as a song and recorded by **The Bass Mountain Boys**, a Bluegrass Band co-founded by my brother Mike. It was the title song on their **Wood and Stone** album. Nice.*

Big Day for the Twins

On a hot summer day in June, 1954, there was a lot of hustling around the house that Saturday morning. The big day of Stevie and my 5th birthday party had finally arrived. Momma was in the hospital at the time but everyone pitched in to make it happen. I woke up from my nap to find a brand new swing set all put together in the yard. Brenda had bought it on the lay-a-way plan. Bobbie had made each of us a circus cake, complete with tent poles and circus animals. And most special to me was the beautiful, long gown that Aunt Pat and Granny made for me to wear. I remember exactly how it looked. It was a very simple sleeveless white top with a long full skirt of sheer white over pale blue taffeta. All our cousins came and there was even a professional photographer to make pictures of everything. I'm not sure who came up with the idea and plan for such a big birthday party, but I never felt more special in my life.

Stephanie Wilson Boggs
March, 2017

I always thought Vanessa was spoiled but after reading this I not sure anymore.

MEMORIES OF MEALTIME

Life in the House By The Creek was a continuous
learning process. One thing I learned from my
parents and probably the most lasting was the
importance of family. There were a lot of us kids
and growing up we sometimes fought with each
other but we also had each other's back-we were
and are today a pretty close knit family. All too
often family time centered around evening meals
(supper) and Sunday Dinners (lunch). We lived on
what was then called a small truck farm. Daddy
raised hogs, cows, chickens, ducks and a garden
big enough to feed the 82nd Airborne. Daddy
always provided for us and taught us how to
provide for ourselves. Teaching us how to hunt
and fish, how to make homemade sausage and
cook Brunswick stew in the big black pot in the
backyard and oh yeah raise enough vegetables to -
well you know. These life lessons are priceless
and have been passed down to our own kids. We
always had enough to eat and Momma made sure
the hot food was hot and the cold food was cold.
What a blessing. Many memories were made over
the years at our large "picnic style dining table"

and having one of Momma's home cooked meals. Some of the best ones are still being made when my brothers, sisters, nieces & nephews all come together for meals, remembering Momma and Daddy and their lesson of the importance of family and togetherness.

Stephen "Stevie" Wilson

For those readers who know Stevie "Rooster" you are probably saying "ain't no way Stevie wrote that", to which I say you're right. He did however, after some prodding from his wife and daughter share his thoughts which his daughter put on paper. Thanks Ashley and thanks Stevie for sharing.

School of Life

Growing up in the house by the creek was definitely a learning experience for me. There were always so many children around. I had eleven brothers and sisters ahead of me and by the time I was two, nieces and nephews were starting to arrive.

Every day was like being in school, I'm just not sure which lessons were being taught and believe me, I'm still trying to figure that out.

I watched my sisters and tried to be like them. Still try to this day. I was amazed at how beautiful they were and could do most anything. Bobbie was like a second mother to me. I was six when Brenda got married and I wore the most beautiful dress I ever had. I felt like a princess. Linda Kay and I shared a bed and I was the one who got in first on those cold nights to warm the covers. Stephanie and I were closer in age and we fought like sisters do. She always had an excuse to get out of washing dishes.

My brothers, now that's another story entirely. The tricks they played on me I can't even begin to describe but they loved me and had my back.

I've heard all my adult life that I was spoiled because I was the baby. Yes, I guess I was. Momma and Daddy gave me a lot of extra attention because I was their last baby.

I was lucky to have the great teachers I did. Momma and Daddy taught me integrity, honesty, hard work and respect. My brothers and sisters taught me how to stand up for myself and to get the things in life I want I had to get them myself. Don't wait for someone else to get them for me.

Great teachers teaching great lessons in The School of Life by the creek. I'm tested every day and just hope I pass when the final exam comes.

Vanessa Wilson Mullinix

Yes Vanessa you were spoiled but I think you'll do just fine on your finals.

The Twins

In June of '49 I was 9 years old,
a real surprise was coming but we hadn't been told
Mama lay on the couch she could hardly bend
But no one suspected she was carrying twins.
A trip to the doctor and then the drug store
For a special concoction of mainly castor oil.
It worked every time she was on the way
In just a short while came Stephanie Faye.
The Doc thought that was it- but to his surprise
Ten minutes later Stephen Ray arrived. The news
traveled fast we were jumping with joy, sister
Bobbie claimed the girl I had to take the boy.
The day they came home I'll never forget
We'd beg to hold them with each little fret.
At five weeks old we all went to the beach
In that big blue basket they were easy to reach.
Months went by and Stephanie decided to crawl
But Stephen just sat and usually bawled.
He finally decided he needed to move
And with a different technique found his groove.
He pulled with his legs sitting straight up
Severely calloused his calves but could have won a
world cup.
We thought he'd never walk without using his
hands, but at 16 months he decided to stand.
Look out world they are wide open now
That they made it this far we all wondered how.
There were battles at home and war in the rice
fields,

Wrecks in the night it's a wonder they weren't killed.

But by the time they were twenty things started to slow down, there were weddings and children and lots of family around.

Life is like a revolving door it takes some out but it brings in more.

There has been lots of this over fifty years

But there are other things that bring louder cheers.

Health and happiness a life filled with joy

But the icing on the cake is Grandchildren galore.

Happy Birthday

Love Brenda

This was written by my sister Brenda for the twins on their 50th Birthday.

Home

It's hard to accept, but the time has come
To sever all the ties
Or better said to loosen knots
Where all our memories lie

Our hearts are full the tears do flow
But we have each other and we must let go

A house is just a place to live
Somehow the warmth is gone
We'll have to find it somewhere else
Alas we're on our own

Pick up the pieces place them well
Don't be afraid to cry
With every tear we heal the soul
It helps us say good-bye

Life can't stop there's more to do
To finish the work begun
We're only a step in the Master's plan
And even with us it won't be done

Written by my sister Brenda in July 1994 seven months after the death of our Mother Violet Mae Wilson. Dad had passed a couple years earlier. When she wrote these lines the house by the creek was empty.

Acknowledgement

I want to thank my brothers and sisters who through the years have given me advice and encouragement. We share a common bond. Our love and respect for our parents and each other drives and unites us in a special way.

I must also thank Don Bolden who was kind enough to edit this book for me. Don and I worked at the Times News for several years and I was really flattered when he agreed to edit this book and write an endorsement for me. Thank you Don.

This book would not exist if it were not for Wayne Drumheller, Editor and Founder of The Creative Short Writers Project. His guidance in design, formatting, legal issues and marketing is priceless. Thank you Wayne.

I owe a large debt of gratitude to all the people who have helped make this book possible. They are the reason for my writing and the inspiration for this book.

Illustrator for cover, Terry Armstrong Hamara
Illustrator for girl on tractor, Nina Hunt
Illustrations by Edwina J. Brown
Eddiebrowne120@gmail.com

About the Author

I don't consider myself an author or poet. I'm just one of twelve children who grew up on a small truck farm on the outskirts of Burlington, NC.
I was born in October 1944, attended schools in Burlington and graduated from high school in 1962. I am sure my English teacher would be just as surprised as everyone else that I have written what I call "stories that rhyme". After high school I joined the US Air Force serving from 1962 until September 1966. After service I worked a year in the grocery business until I was persuaded by my girlfriend at the time to go to college. Elon College worked out, girlfriend not so much. You know what they say "every poem doesn't rhyme". After graduating college with a BA in Business Administration I went to work for the local newspaper in the advertising department and continued there for nine years leaving to open an advertising agency.
I was lucky enough to have some wonderful clients who supported me for over thirty five years.
I retired from the advertising business and now raise miniature horses. Folks often ask me why I raise miniature horses to which I answer "I don't have a clue, just something I wanted to do. " However there are two young girls in Davidson, N.C. that might have had a hand in that venture.
"Ride around easy, ride around slow, today's only here for an hour or so."

In addition to raising miniature horses I have taken up wood turning and now have a wood shop attached to the horse barn. My loving wife thinks I need a couple more projects, just kidding. So here I am now writing poems or "Stories that rhyme". Go figure.

Charlie Wilson grew up as one of 12 children with parents who taught them to work hard, get an education, love one another and make a good life for themselves as adults.

In those years of growing up he developed a strong appreciation for the simple things in his life...the creek by the house, the little white church, the family dog, making molasses, shelling beans and smoking by the big tree.

He built solid values. I first met Charlie when we both worked for the Times-News years ago.

He moved on to form his own successful advertising agency and made his mark in the business world. He also developed an interest in raising miniature horses and has made a new business from that interest.

I knew Charlie would be successful, but I never imagined he would be a poet.

However, he has made me a believer with this collection of his poetic work in which he recalls the precious memories that formed his life.

Don Bolden, Editor Emeritus, *The Times-News*

Violet and Steven L. Wilson

Charitable Fund

Of The Alamance Community Foundation

All royalties from the sale of this book will be given to the Violet and Steven L. Wilson Charitable Fund Of The Alamance Community Foundation.

Family photo December 1993
First row L-R (the girls) Brenda, Bobbie, Vanessa, Linda, Stephanie
Second row L-R (the boys) Gary, Stevie, Charlie, Mike, Tony,
Benny, Scotty

This photo was taken in December 1993. We had just returned to the House By The Creek after attending our Mother's funeral. It is one of the last photos taken with all twelve of us together and all cleaned up in our Sunday clothes.

Remembrance

These memories could not be shared without remembering those who played a vital part in their making and have since passed. They are my parents Violet Mae and Steven L. Wilson and my three brothers Benny, Gary and Tony as well as my grandparents Bert and Ben Dixon and my great Aunt Annie and great Uncle Bud Dixon.